as the Sparrow flies

Praise for as the Sparrow flies

"This is a beautiful book for the lonely, the grieving, the heartbroken, and those who are healing. As Grace elevates ordinary, everyday experiences of loss and change, friendship and motherhood, we are invited to look life's painful realities right in the face and see love looking back at us."

—CHRISTIE PURIFOY, AUTHOR OF *PLACEMAKER* AND *GARDEN MAKER*

"We need the poets to help us translate our biggest feelings, our worst days, our highest highs our ugliest doubts. Grace wraps language around the pain of friendship fractures, "she didn't have time just then / so I let her go/ hot tears in my throat", the ache of mothering "your roots spread and shred / and break me apart," and all the colors of love, "Holy is the heart that breaks." Whatever you're in the middle of, Grace will keep you company there and help make sense of it."

—LISA-JO BAKER, BESTSELLING AUTHOR OF *NEVER UNFRIENDED* AND CO-HOST OF THE *OUT OF THE ORDINARY* PODCAST

"Grace's poetry is an invitation as welcoming in form and tone as her warm and abundant kitchen table. Her words meet the lonely, the grieving, the spiritually-doubting with compassion and spaciousness. I cried and breathed deep, reminded by every line that our long nights and weary grocery store strolls, our people-shaped losses and our abundant joys, matter."

—SARAH SOUTHERN, WRITER OF THE SUBSTACK "WILD & WASTE"

"I read *as the Sparrow flies* in one sitting, and it is now a new favorite on my shelf. Within these tender pages, I found echoes of my own ache and longing—different in the details, and yet, somehow the same. Grace writes with a wisdom and hope that has been weathered. With every word, she generously holds out her hands, offering us pieces of her humanity. She sits down beside us in the shadows, and with one hand around our shoulders, reminds us how terribly stunning it is to be person, and how infinitely we are held."

—SARAH E. WESTFALL, AUTHOR OF *THE WAY OF BELONGING* & HOST OF THE *HUMAN TOGETHER* PODCAST

"This collection of poems has gripped my heart and won't let go. Imagine reading the Psalms, in all of their yearning and lament, and then realizing that the writer isn't speaking of Old Testament armed battles, but modern-day trials that speak to the reader's experience in new, powerful ways. This was my experience with as the Sparrow flies. As Kelley cries out to God about the loneliness of friendships lost, the trauma of complications in childbirth, conflict within one's spiritual community, and much more, she gives language to some of life's deepest heartaches in ways that brought tears to my eyes and healing to my heart. Several times, I audibly gasped, in awe of how Kelley seemed to know my innermost thoughts for which I haven't yet found words. This poetry is an essential companion for anyone who grieves, anyone who wrestles with God, anyone whose questions feel unanswered. Kelley sits in that in-between space with the reader, giving voice to our most crushing disappointments and then, ever so gently, opening our eyes to the kind, gentle Savior who has never left our side."

— ELLIE HUNJA, AUTHOR OF *BLESSINGS, NEW MOM: A WOMEN'S DEVOTIONAL*

"This is, without a doubt, a debut collection of poetry that deftly explores the depths of love, grief, belonging, and faith, with a deep tenderness and skill. If I were to choose a favourite, then, "a friendly face," would simply have to be the one that reached out to me the most. Her vulnerable description of a young mother, uprooted from her familiar surroundings, walking the aisles of the grocery store simply in search of a friendly face to connect with, moved me deeply. I resonated so deeply with this story. Kelley has the ability to transcend the ordinary details that might separate our stories from those of others with her willingness to be vulnerable and her desire to be seen through her words. Her words are always upheld by her deep faith, but there is no attempt to make this the spine of her work. She so clearly lives what she believes and draws the reader into each poem without force. A wonderful collection!"

—LIEZEL GRAHAM, AUTHOR, POET, & TEXTILE ARTIST

"In this collection of poems, Grace has pulled back the veil from our deepest humanity - our great sorrows and joys - and revealed what is sacred in betrayal and loyalty, death and birth, hope and longing. These poems masterfully weave Divine love into the stuff of this earth - into gardens, breastfeeding babies, and grocery store aisles - and is for anyone who knows the ache of love."

—ELIZABETH BERGET, POET & WRITER OF THE SUBSTACK "THE BACK OF THE FLOCK"

as the Sparrow flies

Poems by Grace E. Kelley

Artwork by Bethanie Pack

Synthesis Press

as the Sparrow flies

poems

First Published by Synthesis Press February 2024

Cover Artwork: Bethanie Pack

Interior Artwork: Bethanie Pack

Author photo: Jessica Kautz-Stephens

First Edition

ISBN: 979-8-9866022-2-6 (Trade Paperback)

“last breath” was first published by *Fathom Magazine* as part of a larger project entitled “The Breath Between,” posted March 2020.

Scripture references are from the Christian Standard Bible Copyright ©2017 by Holman Bible Publishers.

to my husband Willy,
and our five beautiful children
Ellie, Boaz, Isaiah, Nathan and Jordan;

without you
    I would not know
    how far
    love goes.

         — G.E. Kelley

for Emily —
You have walked through death with me.
May we continue to search for beauty in the ache together.

         — B. Pack

table of contents

a note to the reader

The poems you are about to read are like polaroid snapshots; captured moments in time that are both incredibly specific and somehow still so significant in the present. Without further ado, I wanted to give you a little sneak peek at the scrapbook cover so you know a little bit of what you can expect in these pages.

Some of the primary topics you will see handled in these pages are friendship joys and losses, loneliness and isolation, death, sexual abuse (not handled explicitly), religious trauma, birth trauma, and the incredibly divine joy and heartbreak that is motherhood.

My hope and prayer for you is that as you read these pages, some of which hold experiences that are similar to your own, and some of which are perhaps completely foreign to you—that you will grow in compassionate understanding for both yourself and for others.

Poetry gives language for what often leaves us feeling bereft and speechless. My dearest hope is that my words do this for you, and for those you love, in ways that feel helpful.

With warmest affection,

Grace E. Kelley

"THEY WILL NOT HARM OR DESTROY EACH OTHER
ON MY ENTIRE HOLY MOUNTAIN,
FOR THE LAND WILL BE AS FULL
OF THE KNOWLEDGE OF THE LORD
AS THE SEA IS FILLED WITH WATER."

—ISAIAH 11:9

benediction

to those brave enough to leave their heart strings dangling frayed—
  loneliness will not consume you,
  and unexpected beauty will find you.

to those brave enough to believe in the land from which no Sparrow falls—
  those who have already traveled there
  will testify that your hope is true.

to those brave enough to want to trust, though betrayal still stings sharp—
  you will find your way back to love again;
  I know the dark you face.

and to those from whom love has asked a heavy, aching cost—
  a cruciform love is in fact the closest to Divine;
  He too knows the ache.

and to you:
wherever you are on the journey—
  I am a chaser of sparrows and
  I am the Sparrow, and
    I wrote this for you.

as the Sparrow flies

how do we count
the heartbreaks?

by tears shed?
or sobs that wrap
our bones in ache?

by silent moments where
'should haves' topple the brim
of the void with emptiness?

by the scars we bear (on body or mind)
where Love turned traitor
and Trust was a liar,
leaving us with wounds so deep
we are forever changed?

but as the Sparrow flies—

how do I begin?
how can I even attempt
to name all that has been lost?

I count my losses in the tens of thousands.
and I used to say,
"I want to love so much that it hurts,"

but I'm tired now.

but as the Sparrow flies—

the truth is:
    I don't know how
    to keep going,
    to keep loving—
    or if I even want to.
can't I hide beneath the covers
until this madness is over?

2

these sharp inhales are hard to take,
and yet I must breathe—
before the knife of dawn shanks
its way through my curtains again.

the way the world just
keeps on turning can feel
like violation,
like violence,
to those whose sheets have become a shroud,
where the broken heart has laid to rest
    —one last time.

but as the Sparrow flies—

my heart is made for Love,
and yet I can hardly remember
the last time she made me tea.
only, how I burned my hand
where I tried to grasp the kettle.

I wonder if someone is keeping track.
is someone out there making sure all this adds up?
hadn't I better spend my heart and money
on something more practical?
a weighted blanket perhaps.

over Distance—
through Death—
in Wounds—
    is there something
    Divine
in this ache?

does Love
look different

as the Sparrow flies?

over Distance —

outsider

I used to walk into rooms
where everyone knew me and loved me.
I felt so valued—so seen,
and how exactly am I supposed to replace the loss
of a decade of friendships?

they weren't perfect of course,
not a one of them.
but they were mine,
and I was theirs,
and now I feel untethered.

I don't belong here.
I don't belong there—
not anymore.

on my children's first day
at their new school in our new town
I stood at the chainlink fence at pickup time.
my head swiveled this way and that, looking
for someone—anyone—begging
with my eyes for someone to see me,
for someone to say, "hello."

if I caught a glance, I'd smile
meaning well,
and well-meaning, the stranger might
smile back—but that was it.
I'd been brushed off
an outsider
and they had a friend with them
already.

I was the homeschool kid showing up
for the first day of fourth grade
at platte river academy
all over again.

by the chainlink fence I stood alone,
desperately scanning,
assessing the light in their eyes,
the curve of their lips,
the sounds of their laughter—

desperately searching
the lines of every face
for a friend.

a friendly face

I was always one to avoid talking to strangers
until the icy blast of a midwest winter
stole my breath away, and I found myself loitering
in the natural foods aisle of the woodman's.

"that one is the best," I'd say to the stranger
looking at my favorite gluten-free brand.
"really? thanks!" she'd reply.

if I was lucky,
the conversation would continue,
and I'd learn that her sister was gluten-free
and would soon be visiting
from out of town.

other days I was not as lucky.
and the loneliness howled,
pushing through the cracks
and chinks in my weak siding,
threatening to put out the fire beneath.

so I cracked a smile at the people standing at the checkout counter.
usually, it was the checkers who would talk to me saying,
"do you need any help out today?"
to which I'd politely reply, "No, I'm okay!"
even though I was not.

one week, a guatemalan abuela visiting her son
was ahead of me in line,
and though she spoke no english,
her smile wrapped around me like the thickest woven blanket
as she clucked and cooed over my precious baby girl,
reaching out a weathered hand to stroke her pale blonde head.

"no mama!" her son sighed, eyes blaring in apology.
"you can't just touch a stranger's baby!"
and maybe she didn't understand,
or maybe she chose not to understand—
but her tenderness warmed me for weeks.

one night I shopped too late
because we needed bread.
my husband offered to go,
but I said I'd do it.

the store was quiet and nearly empty,
as I pushed my squeaky-wheeled cart
down the natural foods aisle
alone
while the winter wind screamed outside.

only the self-checkout lanes were open that night,
maybe because of the weather?
and I wept
as I loaded my bags in my freezing car,
balancing the broken trunk door on my head
because it never stayed open in the cold.

if someone had asked me that night -
"did you find everything
you were looking for?"
I would have said,
"no."

I hadn't gone there for bread.
not really.

frost

I called her on the phone,
my heart an aching mess,
the loneliness suffocating—
the space between us
had taken its toll.

but something she said
had me feeling
she didn't have time just then;
so I let her go,
hot tears in my throat.

she called me back a few minutes later saying,
"that goodbye
sounded a bit frosty—"
and it was all the invitation I needed
to tell her how I was not okay.

because she cared enough
to call me out,
to call me back,
when I was short and angry
with her just for living
her full life
        without me.

angry with her
that she was busy
and I was
        alone.

I thought it meant she didn't care.

but she was the only one
who traversed the 1,000 miles
to milwaukee that year—
despite the promises
of several others.

I counted down
the months,
the weeks,
the days,
until I could take her to kopp's
for frozen custard
and burgers
the size of your face.

and now the only frost
that dares to stand between us
are the cups of frozen custard,
or the affogatos my husband makes,
or the pints we buy in the fog and rain
when we happen to visit prince edward island.

which is to say—
only the sweet kind.

sewn
for Jess

he's sewn you
into my heart
with threads of love
and trust.

when I first heard
you were going away
I felt my heart
would break—the threads
were sewn so tightly.

how your friendship
mended places in me
I didn't know
were torn!

I wonder will I
tear again when
you have gone?

one thing I know for sure:

I will carry the mark
of loving you
like a loose thread,
dangling frayed
all the days
of my life.

best

for Sheila

I saw her in the lobby
of the children's wing,
and like a moth for a fading flame,
I pulled close, and I wept.

"I don't know why
God is taking me
away from you—"

"because,"
 she said, silver standing
at the rims of her blue eyes,
"that's what's best."

and all you need to know
is that only she
could have said
those words to me.

circles

I am moving
in small circles
lately.

from the table to
the dishwasher;
from the front door
to the mailbox.

I rarely need a shoe
other than my well-worn
slippers.

I am carving new paths
away from my illusions
of control and
invulnerability.

they say these days we are lost
and we are found—but mostly,
we are all of us
alone.

the Distance may be the next door over
or a few miles down the road—
it doesn't matter.
right now, those well-worn paths
may as well be
100,000 miles of desert road.

I'm so thirsty.

but I stick to my circles,
looking up and around,
out the same kitchen window,
at the same bookshelf,
the same pilling blue couch—

day to day I circle in sameness
watching everything change.

tightly

lately,
I find myself wondering
why it is that all those souls
who would help me if they could
are a thousand miles away?

the marco polo Kaitlin sends me on a bad day,
the flowers Eryn sent during the dark days of the pandemic,
the voicemail left by my friend Sarah on the day my grandma died,
these are incomparable gifts.

but—

sometimes you just need
a pair of arms
wrapped tightly
around your aching ribs.

the last day

by the time
it was time to leave,
I told the friends I could
to spread the word
that we'd be at the church on sunday.

the church that had loved us
and brought us into its fold
when we were young and tender,
so newly folded together.

I'll never forget the kindness of the faces
of those friends—the girls' night I was invited to
immediately, just because to be there
was to be included.
those years gave me so much joy—
ten years where I grew and learned
to love like a reckless wind
rattling autumn leaves.

but the last day—
maybe we'd just failed to get the word out.
with two six-week olds, I was too tired
to try very hard.

but on the last day
we looked around,
and there was no one there
to say goodbye.

the ghost

I think I became a ghost,
by mistake.

or perhaps, as they say,
I ghosted.

did I forget to say,
"goodbye,"
to you?

or did you text me,
only to receive
no reply?

please know
I didn't mean
to leave you hanging
on a fluttering thread—

but the grief had hallowed me out, scooped all the light out of my eyes and
shoved me with a rough hand out that door—the loose fabric of my pale night-
gown snagging on a splintered shard of wood near the knob, no shred of me
left except this barest trace of this place where I'd spent an age, and I couldn't
defend myself from the onslaught—two mewling babes held tight to my milk-
stained chest, my thin gown barely concealing the gaping wound in my belly,
my heart—and three wraith-light sets of footsteps trailing softly behind me,
holding on to the torn and frayed edges of my fluttering gown, their small fin-
gers fisting around this last certainty—

what I'm trying to say is
it's nothing personal.

perhaps I became a ghost
by mistake.   18

or perhaps, as they say,
I ghosted.

perhaps a ghost
just doesn't have
what it takes
to reach back.

Queen Anne
for Laura

I'll never forget how you told me that you
were probably moving to Georgia in six months,
sitting on the sun-drenched couch in the college apartment
you shared with your military husband.
(we were both so young.)
then, as if reading my mind, my heart—
you shared how you'd learned to make the most of all the time.

I'll never forget how I went against all that screamed within me,
about getting attached, about letting go—
how I chose to pursue our friendship—imagining I knew
what I stood to lose. (I had no idea.)

you've been Anne to my Diana for 12 years now.
and the fire has burned us both—
both of us scorched by refining fires so hot
it made us sweat to sneak a glance in the other's direction.

through the days when I was cold and distant, or our phones weren't talking,
and we both thought the other was angry for some unknown reason—

through the church heartbreaks, and the theological ruptures, the health
scares, and the marriage struggles—

through all the times we have accidentally ghosted each other or double
booked when making plans or had to cancel at the last minute—

through the deaths of loved ones and the deaths of our former selves and
through the endless piles of shit we call our healing journey—

I still make you a cup of tea (unless I'm pouring the tequila), and I always
keep a bottle of gluten-free soy sauce in the house because—

I love every part of you.

every loud announcement from the other room of our airbnb, letting me know with more than a modicum of humor, that you are, in fact, awake.

every exclamation of "SUUUUUUUUUCCCCKKK" when you accidentally drop something. every whipping of your curly head in the charming prince edward island breeze. every excited inhale as you spot a fox crossing the road. (these are only a few things.)

remember that time we couldn't figure out how to put gas in our mini cooper at 4 a.m. and almost missed our flight? both of us directionally challenged and letting google lead us on some backwoods road to hell instead of the u-turn that would have taken us to the airport?

your arms are where I go when I need a reminder that I am cherished. your presence on the other end of the phone, where I retreat to, when I have nothing left, and no one else can bear the sight of all the ugliness in me. you hold it like a precious thing, with fire in your eyes. your anger makes me feel safe and seen and loved. how often does that happen?

I'll do better than Diana, whose love seemed to falter in the end. I'll stand beside you like a warrior sister—like a Queenly friend. I will proclaim your title:
"Defender of the Innocent," from any surface where I'm allowed to stand.

sometimes I think the ones that hurt us would be scared to see us now. maybe if they had known what we were made of, they would have thought twice.

I know now what I couldn't know all those years ago in that college apartment—
we have a bond that no Distance could break.

Queen Anne and the Goddess Diana are perhaps more than simply bosom friends.

I know now we were brought together by more than mere chance or happenstance.

You are the friend I would swim in the freezing North Atlantic with.

these refining fires have become for us a forge—
the hilt and the blade.
the bow and the arrows.

I don't know what battles we still have left to face.
but I know that all that has come for us, looking like destruction,
has failed to do more than strengthen what lies between us.
with you I can look at life and say,
"do your worst."

despite the Distance
for Alli

it's 4,035 miles from here
to the small fishing village
of pucusana, peru.

you have bought two floors
of an apartment building,
and you've bought the land
for the school for children
from the barrios
because you see beautiful
souls who deserve safety
and choices where
governments only see
numbers on paperwork.

miles, measurements,
statistics, and calculations seem
to give information enough
to control—(I fall into it too
sometimes.)
why else
would I count
the miles?

but what I can't work out
is if 4,035 miles
really feels far away—

or if the closer my heart gets
to your dreams,
the closer we become
despite the Distance.

while it is still dark

before golden light crests the hill behind my house,
I see a dozen small sparrows hopping through the shallow snow
in the predawn dark of my backyard.

they are bold, almost cheeky, as they peck their way
through the dry grass and weeds and shriveled crabapples
that have fallen from our tree.

I have heard that He is aware of every feather and flap,
and not one has fallen apart from His notice.
I realize He must know which weeds provide the best seeds,
and He plants these in summer's abundant heat.

these dozen small sparrows do not wonder
who will feed them their daily bread.
it is still dark while they sing their songs of joyful trust,
knowing a feast has already been prepared.

then there's me—with my tear-stained face
pressed to the ice cold window pane,
hoping & praying, for a small sparrow's faith.

through Death—

the other side

waking up
to news of you not waking up—
it never gets easier.

not even if you were 85,
not even if I'd only just learned of your existence,
or all those tragedies that lie somewhere in between.

all that matters is
that you mattered,
and now you're gone.

and it doesn't feel real.
my body wants to reject the wave
of this grief. I cannot bear
to go beneath the waves—
not again.

and I say those words,
not again,
as though I don't know that life is fragile
and precious and impossible to control or predict.

it feels like insult.
like injury.
and I know in some way,
it is both.
but also—

there is a picture in my head
of a desert and an oasis,
a lake glassy and pure, crashes
over a rocky cliff to a pool below.

I am sitting nearby
beneath the shelter of a cottonwood tree,
and you are laughing and splashing
your way up to the waterfall.

perhaps you reached your hand in first,
the water pouring over your skin in sparkling rainbow rivulets.
or perhaps you stepped through the crashing water
all at once.

but I?
I sat up straight beneath the shade of the cottonwood,
and leaping to my feet,
I ran to see the place where you'd gone.

there was no trace of you.

but I can still hear you laughing,
just there—
on the other side.

last Breath
February 20, 2014

6:00 a.m.—
silence descends,
but don't be fooled,
this is not the end
of anything—No.

this is
the pause,
the rest,
the Breath
drawn deep into the lungs—

first Breath, a gasp
a cry unsure

where am I and
what am I and
what in the world?

last Breath—a new birth
into a strange new country
without tears, or fears, or years—

here I am
with the I AM
and oh it really is
True.

she smiles full and with a gleam
in her brown eyes that we have only
hazy seen—through clouds of grief.
woes of worlds weighty on her
drooping shoulders.

now—

now she sees.
and it's not at all like
newborn sight,
blurry and unsure
of arms in which we are held

but close and clear,
and the pleasure is so sharp
perhaps it almost burns
like the light of the lamp
in my newborn's eyes
only—this new birth
doesn't start with a cry

(that is the old way of things)

here, the last Breath
is the pause
for the inhale

before the Laugh.

the house of Grief

the house of Grief smells
like bacon in the pan,
where the Daughter cooks
for the Mother who lost
her own Mother yesterday.

the lights are low
as if the Grief
cannot be seen this way—
as if the space
this woman of faith filled
could be left, ignored in shadows

the Daughter stands
over spitting bacon
and chopped peppers,
and she stirs frantically,
hoping the smell of the bacon
can drive the thoughts
of what it must be like
far, far, away.

when all we project
in the future is loss,
like a dark night
with no moon or stars—
how could we be
unafraid?

projecting fear
is easier than
anticipating joy—
one imagines loss
and builds a fortress
'round a wounded heart

the other sees
the bird at the window
as a messenger of hope
that devastates all else.

the black-eyed junco

I stand at the door
and knock
like the black-eyed junco
tapping
at the back glass door
since the day before yesterday.

in the afternoon
she appeared,
like a herald of comfort
we didn't know we needed.
like a sign of provision
when we didn't know our lack.

Grandma died
later that evening,
and Gamamma sent a sign
to tell us she was near—
a black eyed junco tapping
at the back glass door.

tap
tap-tap-tap
tap-tap

like she was
desperate to get in,
desperate to comfort,
desperate to remind us
of the One who stands
at the doors of Grief
and knocks.

the Anvil (I.)

loss is like
an Anvil
sitting silent on my chest.
the only noise comes
when I try
to breathe.

the creaking of my lungs
fighting to expand in this
weighted world
sounds like the rattling
of chains softened
by padded walls.

words pad the cell:
    "she lived a good life."
    "it was her time."
    "she was ready."

AND IF I COULD ONLY STAND I'D RIP THAT PADDING OFF THE WALLS
AND DASH MYSELF AGAINST THE COLD AND SOLID REALITY THAT
DEATH IS ALWAYS AN UNINVITED AND GREEDY HAND AT THE TABLE
AND THERE IS NO EXCUSING HIM.

I have tried to move
the Anvil
by ignoring it,
pretending that I believe
padded words
are enough to quench
embers burning
a hole in my chest
where my heart used to be.

but
surprise, surprise!
it didn't work.

after sitting in the numbed silence
for 100 more years, I took another
rattling breath—my lungs like a bellows
on the embers of a heart gone
almost cold as I whispered—

"I didn't get to say goodbye."

and the anger lifts the Anvil—
throws it broken to the ground.
and I do as I said I would;
tearing padding, dashing
every part of me against the cold,
hard stone until
either my bones
or the wall
must break.

is this what they call a tragedy?

remember when we heard in school
that tragedy meant
"the singing of the goat"
and we laughed?

how ridiculous it seemed.
how totally unrelatable.

but have you ever heard
a mother goat bleating
for her lost kids?

I have.

and these children
were not being led to the slaughter
on the altar of a false god
for a pagan feast or festival,
but she didn't know that.

she only knew
that all at once
they were gone.

I reached for her golden ears
when she paced by me, frantic.
I tried to soothe away the fear.
I tried to tell her of the meadow
where they'd gone to run,
and the horses with whom
they'd learn to play.

but she didn't understand.
couldn't understand.
couldn't believe me
even if she did.
instead, she just stood
at the locked gate and stared,
looking at the place she'd seen them last
and bleating out her sorrow.

Why is it

Why is it
so hard
to believe
that I will see them again?

the sliver

there was a sliver in my hand—
I don't know of what.

perhaps wood from the handle of the broom,
or glass from what I swept up yesterday,
or a piece of a thistle from gardening.

but in the days before
Grandma passed away it happened
and after—
the sliver inflamed my hand
with an infection
like grief,
like tears bottled up,
needing a cleansing escape.

and it hurt!
when my husband
brandished a needle
to clean out my wound,
and I yelled words I had never said,
and I cried—

but not about
my hand.

sunscreen

yesterday I got
sunscreen in my eyes.
stinging, blinding me—
I couldn't see.

but when I wept last night
about how I didn't get
a birthday card
from either grandma
this year—

my vision finally
began to clear.

I'm tired of tears

I'm tired of tears
of grief,
of mourning

it's morning here—
when was the joy
supposed
to arrive?

clinging to hope
like a woman
scaling the empire state building
without a rope,
without a harness—

fingers poised white
on the ledge like my life
depends upon it
(and it does.)

after all
one hand slipped,
then the other,
just last year.

I free fell
into despair
like an ocean of asphalt,
hot and sticky,
in my lungs—
sinking from the impact,
eyes no longer
believing in heaven.

that's what happens
when you just can't hold on
to hope anymore.

but I wonder,
if there isn't some other way?
can hope be a rope
around me, someone else
holding on tightly
to me
for awhile

while I'm falling?

I don't like planting seeds

I love to garden,
but I don't like planting seeds.

every year winter's lies
get to me, and I believe
that all is dead and dying.

I can hear the taunts,
as clear as a bell: "do you really believe
there is life in this shriveled up pea?"

I feel like an idiot
worse—
like a fool in love
with spring –
with a lust for life that
consumes my thoughts
and dreams.

but life in the garden
can be disappointing
sometimes too.

my doubt
this year made me
procrastinate,
and I planted my tomatoes
far too late.

and I do not know
if the fruit will mature
before winter's return
this time.

now you are the seed
for Grandaddy: August 2020

now the soil is carved
to make way for hands
that handled seeds with care
all their earthly days.

       now you are the seed—

once you made space
for what looked like Death.
for dried soy beans and
shriveled corn—
dusty field peas and string beans,
turnips, collards, and more.
(even tobacco seeds—for better
or worse)

       now you are the seed—

once, you sowed faith
small as grains of mustard
into three small hearts,
      and by grace like rain
they grew.

once, you held grands and great-grands
in your weathered hands—
and by grace like rain,
      we will grow to sow faith
like you.

       now you are the seed—

now, I need the faith
of a farmer like you

to nestle you gently
in borrowed earth
like Paw-Paw's sweet potatoes
so carefully arranged—
to plant the seed of you
beside the one for whom you tended
gardens and roses and feeders full of hope
like birdseed.

now, I need the faith
of a farmer like you
to disbelieve what my eyes
have seen
and believe instead
in fields of glorious green and songs
of eternal spring—the land
from which no sparrow
falls.

now you are the seed
in the hands of a Farmer
even older and wiser than you—

and He knows
the time to plant.

and He knows
the harvest
is coming.

now you are the seed
we sow in tears—
but we will reap
with shouts of joy.

Life Forever

why so sad?
not gone—
not far—
just there!
beyond the veil,
beyond the view of what human
eyes in earthly sight can see

(as the Sparrow flies)
not gone,
not far—my Soul
why weep?
why wail?

don't you know
the end of this story?
has it not been told to you
from the beginning?

was it not she
who took you upon her knee
and whispered truths
magnanimous and more magical
than any fairy tale—

from a book of worn leather
and frail pages, white and thin
as her wrinkled skin—

stories of a King
who died for the girl he loved,
so they could be together
forever?

who knew—this Death
was the Path towards
Life
Forever
for them both?

the Anvil (II.)

blind and wounded,
is this how we come?
crashing through that solid
wall of reality,
my bones turned to powder,
my eyes gritty,
my nostrils full of dust
and funeral ashes.

lying under a bright
and open sky—
the beauty sharp
like grief—
at first felt worse

than the anvil
that sat on my chest
1000 years—a weight
—where my heart
used to be.

and now this?!

as I crashed through the walls
to the truth that Death
was always just a door
out of the tower,
out of the nightmare,
out of the shadowlands

to Here—
where air is breathed
just for
Laughing.

beyond this shadow's edge

I know now what it will be like
when the veil between our world,
and the next, vanishes completely.

on wednesday, the warbling voices
of (more than a few) off-key children
rose in cheery Christmas tunes
from the depths of our small school's gymnasium.
and the hardest part for the children
was not the singing as you'd expect—
but instead the impossible restraint of singing
without lifting their arms above their eyes
to peer through the over-bright green and red
stage lights and into the audience beyond.

more than one of them failed in this restraint,
(my own children among them) but quickly remembered themselves
and lowered their arms again—still unseeing.
and you could feel the gathering frustration
building in their tiny bodies:
>   are they out there?
>   are they watching?
>   what do they think of me now?

when the final song came to a cheerful close,
they gave it up altogether.
every child had his or her arm above their eyes, sparkling and unsure,
peering out into the black,
stage blinded and still unable
to make out more than a few meager shapes.

then all at once, someone flipped on the light.

for a moment, we held our breath,
letting the children find us
in the crowd, their eager eyes
scanning faces with hope and determination.
and though we had already been clapping
as the children gave their final bow,
once more the thunder of applause
filled the echoing gymnasium,
and once more there rose the whoops,
hollers, and whistles of unbridled joy:
> *you did it!*
> *we saw you!*
> *we are so proud of you!*

I stood in the back, and couldn't stop the tears from coming
my children's faces fixed on my own—
for the joy of being seen at last
for where I had been all along.

and it struck me like a lightning bolt
that just beyond this shadow's edge,
I too am watched by those who wait
for the light to be flipped on –
those witnesses in the cloud
have yet to stop cheering for me.

and I feel sure of it now,
one day I will hear the sweet sounds
of their clamorous applause
and shouts of raucous joy—
their pride over me chasing away
the failures and fears
of my imperfect song.

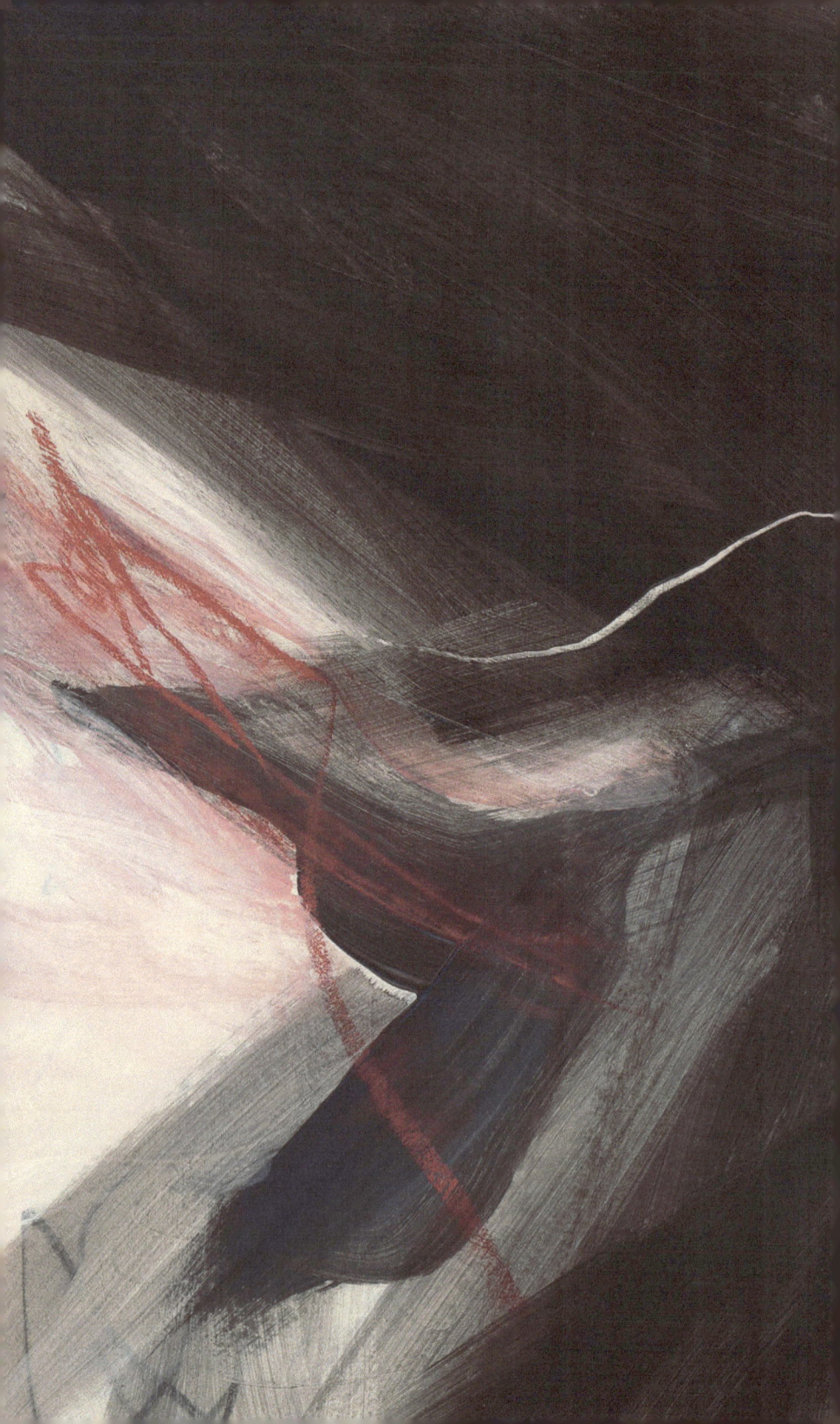

in Wounds—

can the Sparrow fly

can the Sparrow fly
from here to Hades—
or wherever you've been
keeping your soul
lately?

or is this the Distance
that cannot be traversed
even by Death?

to joint and sinew,
of holding up
these weights, this marrow
is aching with the pulse
of blood always asking more
from me.

appetite for life was mine
once—
              I was very young,

and the yellow forsythia covered in dew
made my bare toes wander.

but that was before.

sometimes now I feel old—
old & older than I ever
thought possible,
              and still so far to go.

I am 27 until tuesday,
but still I feel these bones
are wearing out
and down,

rocks turned to sand
by the beating of the waves,
beaten down and away
and I—
              the last one on the shore;
so proud, so sturdy—

the last one to be beaten
down and away,

and what sorrow is now mine,
now that I too,
am wearing away.

maybe I could be her again—

my chest aches, and
they don't tell you about the pain of desire!
or the weight of these bones
while yellow forsythias bloom with light!

can't I just shrug it all off—
toss my balled up socks
in the direction of the backdoor
on my way out?

would I
feel the dew making light
of these weary bones
in my bare toes,

making them light
enough to dance?

my body is a House

my body is a House
you broke into.

you smashed the window,
threw open the door—
you stomped through
every room with muddy boots,
and rearranged my furniture.
you flicked ashes on the smooth pine
of my perfect floor,
burning holes as you went.

after you left,
I tried to tell Her
She was safe.

I scrubbed the walls—
replaced the window,
changed the locks.
I returned the furniture
to its proper place
and covered the holes
with an area rug.

but when car lights
swing through my windows
at night—I feel your hands
at the keyhole,
and I know
what happens once
can happen again,
and how can I
stop it?

my body is a House,
and I can still smell
the stench of your violation.
my walls crawl with memory.
no paint can cover the smell
of cigarette smoke
penetrating every room.

(at least now
I know where most of the holes
in the pine planks are.)

my body is a House,
and where have I hidden
myself?

in the attic—
cramped and dark.
the heat and fear
make my sweat stink.

but I can't come out.
not now. not ever.
    —even with the locks changed.

because my body is a house,
and it's clear
it's not *my* House
anymore.

broken spine

I don't mind a book
with a broken spine,
the edges of the pages already
thumbed through and ragged,
a dog ear or two can put me
quite at home.

I don't mind
the scratches on top
of my washing machine.
it's sort of nice actually
having those first
imperfections out of the way.
it helps me let the rest go.

when we moved into our house
and bought a new-to-us refrigerator for $400,
the struggle to get it through
the doorway left it with a gouge
on the freezer door.
and my husband felt bad,
but I told him—
if the scratch had been there before,
I still would have bought the fridge.

it's what's inside that counts.

and I'll tell it to you, my friend,
who feels worn out
and used, and who carries the baggage
of all those past relationships.
how beautifully they began,
and how terribly they ended—

I hope you know
I don't mind
a broken spine.

I'm broken in places too,
and scratched up, and dog eared,
and some of the notes in my margins
misunderstand me completely.

truly, I don't mind
the broken—

so long as I
haven't done
the breaking.

plot twist

I knew it was over
when I saw you standing
by the coffee counter—
your arms were full of
books I had lent you.

you twisted a knife in my gut
when you stretched out
your arms to return
what you thought
you owed me.

after years of gentle use,
of dog-eared pages,
and highlights,
and scribbles in the margins
of joyful exclamations—

you returned
my affections,
my trust,
my friendship,
like an unwanted gift.

perhaps
you didn't know
what to do with it.
but I don't remember
giving you a receipt.

now, am I supposed
to return home and
put you on the shelf—
to forget about the ending
of the plot twist
I never saw coming?

black hole

I am walking
wounded— a black
             hole
in the center
of my chest.

most people
don't see it;

my smile, my laugh—they cover
nicely, like my colorful shawl
from jerusalem or
the scarf I got in france.

It started off small—
a pinprick, maybe
a dot of darkness
where a star used to be.

then bit by bit
and piece by piece,
the edges have been
caving in,

slowly some days
and quickly others,
it grew four sizes
two months ago—

            I cannot tell you why.

now it makes up
most of my chest cavity.
(and you would know
if you could see.)

and you would think
there would be terror
in the face of such
destruction
        —but no.

my heart is all-consumed,
too consumed,
to keep
caring—

heartbreaks
too innumerable
will do that
to you.

I
am
going
numb.

I
have
a
black
hole
in
my
chest.

can
you
see
it?

—ouch!
back away!!

look at this shawl
my mother-in-law
bought me in
the holy land.

but please—
admire from
a distance.

I would hate
to suck you in.

your love is like

your love is like a fire
in the outdoor grate.

warm and so beautiful—
until the wind
blows ashes on my dress,
and smoke makes my eyes
sting and weep.

(love is like that
sometimes.)
the tears come, and maybe
it's no one's fault—

but here I am
            weeping.

and I could leave
the circle of your warmth
if I wanted to—
but I don't.

instead I'll cover my
eyes with my sweatshirt
sleeve and hope
you overlook these tears
when the wind finally
shifts direction.

I thought you were dead.

I thought you were dead.
it was the only thing that made sense.

the elders walked onto the stage,
and you were not among them.

I thought you were dead.
it was the only thing that made sense.

I knew the meeting was nothing good;
perhaps there'd been a tragic accident?

I thought you were dead.
it was the only thing that made sense.

like smoke, the fear of hundreds
stuffed itself down my tightening throat.

I thought you were dead.
it was the only thing that made sense.

but then they told us what you had done:
the double life you lived
while we rested our hearts
in hands that lied & stole & cheated—
    oh how you cheated!

and all I could think was
"it can't be true;
no, he must be dead."

and all at once I realized,
I would have preferred it that way.

(I know that sounds dark,
and I'm sorry.)

I don't wish you were dead,
 but—
it would have made more sense.

you could hear
    gasps—
    sighs—
the sniffs & sobs tore
their way from my throat
as I lay my head down
on the wooden pew—
a heart too buried
and broken
to stand.

our trust broken,
our community betrayed,
you loved your sin more
than those you claimed to love.

you worshipped yourself
more than the God
who made you.

but He is still here—
even if you are not.

His words are true
even if yours are not.

He's still the God
who can forgive you
for all you've done

even when I
cannot.

how I feel now

remember how
a few weeks ago
you preached about
the grief we carry
for others?

with compassion
in your eyes
and tears in mine
—I thanked you.

but I'd like you
to imagine
how I feel
now:

under the weight
of grievous corporate,
communal, and yet
deeply personal
grief—

worse than a death,
this loss of who
we thought you were.

how can we
recover
now?

can you imagine
how I feel
now?

the face of my friend?

I saw your face
in a photo yesterday,
a harmless little photo
on a facebook page.

but the tears came hot
and sudden as I realized
the transformation:

the face of my friend
has become the face
of a stranger.

I didn't want to look at you
in the shock of the aftermath.
the revelations too horrible—
I glared at the back of your head
from the other side of the room.

but today I wish it was your voice
telling us it is all going to be okay—
the voice I have loved,
the eyes I have trusted,
the hands that made us feel safe again.

today I want to ask:
"how could you?"
and for you to somehow
tell me something
that makes sense.

for you to tell me
that my friend
is still in there
somewhere.

to protect you

I don't want to tell
people what's happened
now—

I feel a shame
like I should
have known—

like I gave
my heart & trust
away too
foolishly.

but also,
I still love you.

and a part of me
wishes all this
weren't true.

a part of me
(unimaginably)
wants to protect
you.

the Difference

I think I know now
how the disciples felt
as they watched the backs
of Judas and Jesus
amidst the clutch
of roman spears.

the betrayal so sharp
and stabbing, like a blade
between the ribs.
like a man hauling
himself up on nails
to get a breath—
to ask for a drink.

were you giving us vinegar
when we asked for wine?

could we really
not tell
the Difference?

(im)possible us
for Alli

I remember the day
I saw you walk by—
and (im)possibly,
we weren't friends.

I couldn't see your eyes
behind your sunglasses.
my body stiffened
beneath my backpack,
weighty as worlds we thought
we'd be living in together—
but now apart.

a few months later
you (im)possibly asked
me to meet you
in the dining hall.

(I didn't want to go.)
I was scared of
what you might say.
Something told me
to go anyway.

I twirled my pen
above my journal—
like your invitation wasn't
every (im)possible reason
I was there—like every piece
of me sitting in that plastic egg chair
wasn't desperately hoping
for an outcome I didn't
believe in.

but when you said:
    "I'm sorry. I miss you."
and I said:
    "I forgive you. I miss you too."
I realized that you
were the more faithful
of us two.

even in your anger
you kept me safe
on sidewalks when buses you
could have pushed me under
came regularly and often,
and when I was pushed
beneath wheels by others,
it was you who stooped
down low, brushed dirt
off my face, and told me
truths I no longer believed.

it was more
than I had done
for you.

your sunglasses sat
on that grey formica table
between us, your brown
eyes the ones I remembered
sharing sorrows and joys with
for all my most formative years;
your humble breath
between us giving
living air to the lungs
of a friendship
I thought was
(im)possibly dead.

you resuscitated us—

when walking away
was all I knew how to do,
and how can I thank God enough
for you?

now it is your breath
that fills my lungs
when I say,

"(im)possible things
do happen."

I was wrong
for Tamara

I thought it was over
that day
when I read your letter.
I got into the shower
and cried for an hour.

I no longer remember
what it said.
but the feelings
of devastation
remained with me
for years.

until that day
when you sent me
another, quite different letter;
asking me,
"where did we
 go wrong?"

and I told you,
"I have already
forgiven you,
there is no need
to rehash all
that is past."

and I told you
I'd like it if we
could be friends
again.

when your dad died
later that year,

something in me
broke open for you.
and I knew
it was more than
I had ever felt for you
in my younger,
more self-absorbed life.

and through the tears
and sorrow somehow
we found our way back
to each other. back
to a friendship old as
monkey bars & tetherball;
older than the Wounds which
caused us at first
to part—

and all I kept hearing
(in my heart or in my head,
I'm not sure) is that

I was so sure it was over.

I would have told anyone,
"and that was how
that ended."

yet here I am now,
living in a future I never
imagined for us;
so full of gratitude

that I was wrong.

the Starling
for Anna

God blew you in
like a starling,
roosting in a bedraggled,
beat up tree,

a sweet young thing
eating away at the bugs
infesting my branches and leaves,
yet leaving the little fruit
well enough alone.

strange it would seem
that you take so little.
and yet I want to offer you
everything, just in hopes
that you might stay
a little longer
in these weathered branches and
tell me of the wild world beyond
these haggard woods in which I find myself.

some days, it seems
this whole wooded world
is ready to catch fire
and crumble down around me—

yet you sit here,
calm as anything,
a watchful look
in your eye—
as if you know
something
I do not.

many somethings
perhaps.

perhaps
there's a world
in your eyes
that I have only
begun
to dream of.

even still
for Willy

people say
       "let's grow old together,"
like it's some pale, pink fluttering thing.
like it doesn't mean
       "yes,
       let's love each other through more
       foibles, flaws, frailties, and failures
       than we even (now) know we possess."

people say
       "we're only friends now—
       we aren't in love (anymore).
       it's over."
and they toss a nuke
on the house with the comfortably stained carpets
and the chipped paint—the good bones ignored
and destroyed forever.
and is there anything more tragic
than giving up on friendship's fire
while small embers burn on,
waiting only for the chance
to leap again into flame?

people said
       "you are too young to know about love."
they were a little right—
but wrong to discourage us.
I know now these lessons
do not come with age.
only time can teach us how to hold on.
your hands around my wrists—
my grip on your strong forearms—
while a tornado whips us around.
unearthing the unspeakable,
upending all that was comfortable,
us watching—our faces strained and pale—
as all we thought we knew
was torn into bits.

that swirling vortex
would have torn us too
by now
            if we'd let it.

but I said to you,
            "no matter what."

I was only 19. But I meant it.

—13 years of marriage
and I love even more about you now than I did then.
the storied paths of laughter and grief
around your eyes welcome me home like an embrace.
the white streaks of your beard are blessed
as the snowy slopes where you first held my hand.
and you? you love the tinsel in my hair,
and the over-risen loaf of my soft middle,
stretched and collapsed with love and life.
not even my scars repulse you.
you say;
            "they just remind me
            that you are very brave."

and the tethers that bind us—
more than those pale, pink flutterings
of romantic aspirations or imaginary
old-aged, happily ever afters:

instead
your hands around my wrists—
my grip on your strong forearms—
and the nail pierced hands
of the God-Man
holding us together,
even still.

the ache of Divine Love.

in the pieces

I'm learning to measure
differently—
by the sparrows,
if you will.

as the Sparrow flies
over Distance,
through Death,
and in Wounds—
time and space expand
and fold
and turn in reverse,
        even now.

I need glasses that do more
than help me see in front of my face
or block the glare of the sun.

I need a way to track her flight
        upside-down,
                inside out,
        behind me,
                inside me—

where I anticipated and where
I never expected her to go.

it's the only way
I can learn to see
this ache
—o yes,
all this ache
is Divine.

those who seek her
with a broken heart
will find her
in the pieces.

river stones

here we are
again—

in that place
where the water
rushes in,
where the sting
of death and sin
comes crashing
overhead
again.

here we are
again—
trying to keep
our heads
above the rapids,
white with angst and
foaming with dirt
and debris.

I've tumbled
head over heels
over head again.
still the water rushes
over me, and I can't tell
which is the way
toward heaven.

but in this
crashing and foam
I have a hope
the shape of
wonder:

is all this
as it seems?

are we being
destroyed?

    or
are we being
worn smooth
like
     river
        stones?

(I must have missed) dancing

I want to find
my way back
to the girl
whose lust for life
made her splash
in rain puddles—

whose love
made her free
as all the birds
she watched
flying south.

lately,
I've been dancing
in my kitchen.

and I say
it makes me feel sexy,
but what I really mean is
that it makes me feel *alive.*

Have I
been gone
so long?

a dead heart
in a chest still breathing?
forgetting
how to laugh—
forgetting
what it means
to exist where both
joy and sorrow do?

I knew that girl once:
the puddle dancer
always laughed
at lightning.

and I loved her—
for all her joy-
full innocence.

then I was made to watch
as the rain
drowned her out.

all at once the water
became deep,
too deep,
to splash in.

for one
terrible
moment
she went under.

but now,
through (albeit clumsy) steps
on my kitchen floor,
I find I'm teaching her
to live again.

now I find,
I'm teaching her
to dance
upon the waves.

resurrection on 287

I've seen

on highway 287

                                               the broken down house

cinderblock walls,
only rafters left for a roof,
a gaping hole where
a once presentable
exterior used to be.

when I drive by

                                               my broken down heart—
though jaded and cynical
by all accounts—

                                                   is filled with brutal
                                                           longing.

I fantasize
about pulling the car over
and rushing to what was once
the doorway and running
my hands over ruined
cinderblocks and wood
until the love of the place
would change it –
like a Resurrection—
a new house from these
crumbled cinderblocks.

                                                       maybe this
                                                   is how I know
                                                 I really do believe
                                                     in all things
                                                      made new—

one day—
my heart like
the cinder block house,
all coarse and rough will be
smoothed out with sandpaper
the walls rebuilt to safety,
the shutters painted,
the door flung recklessly wide—
(because being whole and loved
will do that to you).

and what meals we will share!
in a kitchen once marked by
ash and rubble,
with fruits from the garden
growing wild out back
    just because it can.
there is nothing to stop it.

the broken down house
on 287 reminds me of
what sometimes seems
so terribly easy
to forget—

                                    I really do believe
                                      in Resurrection.

mother's day

on mother's day
I rise early
to ask the violas
how they slept.

to see the marigolds
and verbenas shining
velvety with morning dew.

to ask the snapdragons
and the daisies if they have
enough room.

I listen to the chatter
of the birds singing
glory to the Maker
of the morning
(as they do every day)
without question,
without fail.

I think of how the earth
knows better than I do
how to receive the love
of a God who is both
Father and Mother—
words I am only just
learning how to say.

in the morning light
this day does not feel
tangled up as I know some
(perhaps most) people
feel it to be.

here there are no
mothers abandoning
their children.

here there are no
empty wombs.

here there are no
words spoken
with anything less than
utterly devoted love.

here there are no
tiny graves.

here no arms ache
for the love they used
to hold.

here there are no
women deceived
or forced into life's
most terrible choice.

here there is only
dew on fresh flower faces
and light
and grace
and the God who says
he loves us—

like a mother hen
longing to gather us
beneath protective wings—

like a nursing mother
who cannot forget
the son of her womb
because of the ache
in her breasts—
the nourishment
she must pour out,

she cannot keep it
to herself.

and perhaps what I want
to celebrate today
is not me—

someone privileged to be
a mother
to earthly children,

who holds five hearts in her hands
like the abundance
she knows she doesn't deserve,
a kindness to which
she is neither entitled
nor guaranteed.

perhaps instead I want
to celebrate like the birds
the King of Creation—
the God of the Morning—
who loves me like the child
that I still am.

who loves me so much
it would hurt to turn away.
who loved me

to the point of death
and life again.

the Mother God
who is even now
preparing for me
a feast of welcome
and celebration
when I have done
all my wanderings
in these shadowed
lands.

I catch glimpses
of this and more in the shining
dew-dropped faces
of the violas in sunshine.

in the tears I know
our truest Father
and Mother sheds
for the ache
of us all.

let me be/ your breath

grow in me—

all that is
new and tender,
the unseen seems
more real with each
fluttering sign
of presence.

(the flutters
gave them away
 after all)
—how I knew
they were two
and not only one.
now my desires
are more refined
than ever.

so grow in me—

until the pain
makes it hard
to rise from my sheets,

until I'm
stretched and marred
far beyond
my capacity,

until red stripes
mark my belly,
full and heavy
with the weight

of the glory
of you.

grow in me—

until sleep
becomes
a stranger,

until breaths
feel hard to take—
for the crowding
of my lungs
is no less Holy
than singing
praises to the God
who made you.

grow in me—

until you are ready
to breathe
with fresh lungs—

until the sweet echos
of your first cries
tear open places
always meant
for loving you,

until then,
Dear Ones,
grow in me—

and let me be
your breath.

beneath my ribs

beneath my ribs
two souls bloom
like stubborn shoots pushing
through the cracks
in stones on the mountain side—
spreading, breaking,
then opening
in glorious flower
ignorant of the Ache,
the destruction
they've caused.

my daughter does not know
how her head has strained
a muscle beneath
my left rib cage.

my son does not know
how his toes wedged
between bones
feels to a mother
heavy with the weight
of a beauty not her own.

but I'll be the rock
if you'll be the seedlings
growing precisely
where you are planted.

(I know Who plants the flowers
on the mountain side.)

even if it means
your roots spread and shred
and break me apart,

even if it hurts—
I am learning to embrace
the Ache that makes me
more than just
a stone.

for the love

in august of 2020
in north carolina heat,
a woman holding a child
stepped off the curb in a graveyard
and fell.

she didn't know it was a curb.
she was blinded by tears and
her mask and was tripped
by that impossible lip
of cement in the cemetery
where her grandfather
was being laid to rest.

see her as she falls—
not forward as one might assume,
but rotating,
turning,
curling in
the child close to her chest.

it was instinct that led
to the fracture of her elbow
and the bloodying of her knee
and the embarrassing tossing
of her skirt above her waist.

but the child got up
without a scratch.

and isn't that
what Mothers do?

eleven months later
she gave birth to two babies in
two different ways,
double the pain,
and she?
she endured them both.
for the children—
for the love.

she cried out:
asking for help
asking for relief—
they only asked her
"do you want to go to sleep?"

'NO.' she said, angry
that they suggested it.
disgusted by doctors
and anesthesiologists
who didn't know her
or understand her
or why she said it.

they thought
the pain was not
so bad.

       it was.

but she was the Mother
who turned elbow out
to scrape and fracture
on asphalt
to protect the child.

she the Mother
who kept watch all night
with the child doubled over in pain.

she the Mother
who would lose life and limb
for more than just her blood—
for all she loved—
for the love.

she the Mother
and the daughter of Mothers
who faced court rooms and police officers,
who faced the faces of men they loved
as they turned them away.
who faced illness and fears in foreign lands
for the sake of the few
who faced poverty and abuse for the sake
of those they loved—

SHE— the Mother:

and they saw the inside of her but not all the way inside because if they had, the
fire would have blinded them like the rage she felt when she saw the bruises
on her daughter's arm; the arm they yanked and pulled because they did not,
could not believe in the strength of this Mother and her Daughter and all that
they would become.

SHE—Mother and Daughter
            survived.
her boy too.

her elbow hurts
when the storm comes in
and when autumn arrives.
and her c-section scars ache

with the memory of all
that was done to her.
but she is a Mother.
    and *for the love*
she will do
whatever it takes.

this is my Body

I heard it beneath the fluorescent lighting
of my hospital bathroom mirror
where I shuffled in to use the toilet
for the first time since they ripped
my daughter out of me.

the hollow eyes staring back at me
belonged to a stranger,
and I knew somewhere
deep down, that the me from before
was gone forever.

but when I looked
towards the large white bandage
on the lower half of my still swollen belly
I heard these familiar words:

> *this is my body*
> *broken for you.*

and in a way I never
would have asked for
or expected, I knew
that God had answered
my prayer after all.

"Lord,
show me
how much
you love me."

Divine Love

let me start by giving you
a few examples:

> my husband cradling my scar—
> his wide palms bracing me
> as I wept in my midwife's arms.

> the gentleness with which
> he tended an area of my incision
> that was becoming infected
> until the wound could finally
> begin to close.

> the tenderness with which
> he removed leftover adhesives
> from my bruised and aching belly for days
> after my traumatic c-section.

> the way he rubbed my back each night
> until I could finally fall asleep,
> telling me that I was safe at last.

Divine Love isn't instagram perfect or pretty.
(I don't have a photo of any of this,
but my skin holds the memory.)

love like this is as raw and real as the slash of a scalpel—
as a mother staying awake through horrid pain to be there for her babies—
as a husband holding his wife's hand as she endured the worst,
begging God to take the pain away.

and there are few things that I know for sure, like I know this:
being Beloved of the Divine is both safe and terrifying.

living with a weakness that (somehow) doesn't make me less lovable—
standing firm in a place where my frailties are tended and embraced—
my pain drawing my lover nearer with the tender compassion of the crucified
Christ—

all burning coals of kindness
all heaping piles of grace
I could never hope to repay.

curl close

curl close to me
in the soft center of my body,
in the soft center of my love.

here, you'll find food
and warmth.
let my knees make a cradle
for your feet and
let my right arm guard
your tiny head
while you sleep.

let my left arm
be your blanket
tucking you in close—
almost as close as
when we shared breath.

sense me and feel safe
in the circle of my arms—
the dark of the womb
replaced by the dark of this room
where we sleep,
and you eat,
and I hold these moments
as closely as I hold you.

they won't last.

even so,
curl close to me
as I tuck you in a love
strong enough
to envelop you
for all time.

Anything & Everything

did it hurt?

when Thomas put his child-like
hand into your spear-torn
side—the only cure
for his grown-up unbelief?

2,000 years later
my twins dig their toes
into the wrinkled skin
of my belly stretch-marked
by my love and their growth.
    (I don't mind it so much—)
but it hurts when the tips
of tiny toes find the edges
of the scar from whence
Jordan came, and
sometimes I still feel
the zip of the scalpel
across my tender skin
and feel afraid.

but they seem to seek it
like a reassurance,
like a firm place to stand
amidst a sea of softness.
    (to be feminine is not all
    softness—there is no one more
    ferocious than a mother.)

as if Nathan is trying to remember
the way I roared him earth side
with a power like the tide.

as if Jordan is seeking the strength
with which I held on to hope,
to consciousness, to *her*—
amidst incredible pain.
as if my scar, like an anchor
holds their four tiny feet fast
to this one truth:

I would do anything.

and I think of Jesus 2000 years ago,
his heart broken for the world
then and now— his heart
aching for his friends,
Judas' betrayal still sharp
as a spear jabbing his mind—
his hand tracing the place
where thorns tore the forehead
his mother used to kiss goodnight
as they mocked him—
the memory of the pain
on her beloved face as she stood
there watching him die—
the agony of that last
shallow breath—

    this Jesus
offers his torn open body to Thomas:
like a drink of living water;
like a mother with a milk-stained shirt,
and an open wound,
and a bleeding body,
coming for the crying child
in the dark of night with this
reassurance, this one truth:

I would do anything.

did it hurt?

is the ache still there somedays
in your glorified body
where you chose
to keep your scars?

2,000 years ago
Thomas ran his clumsy fingers
across the edges of your wounds,
and at last the proof sparked
the flame in his eyes—
the light of a child believing
        at last
in his own Belovedness.

and here I am
grasping for the strength
of a childlike belief.

digging my toes in
to this weighty anchor

of a love that did everything.

good company

Holy is the heart that breaks

for the world,
breaks open
in a shattering million
ways each day—
and the heart that held
constellations and comets
committed Himself to carnal death
for love of this world.

Love breaks us open
because His heart breaks
open with Divine Aching
for all the lost souls,
for the pain of this world,
and for all the ones who
still hope to find them.

but one thing
I still hold like a small
child against my chest;
the truth that
this—

this is not
the end—and also;
loving's ache
and every break
find their solace
in the Divine
embrace.

and so, to the me
that I am now, I say,
"find yourself
in good company."

epilogue: not so far

as the Sparrow flies
it's really not so far.

though the Distance parts
and Death severs
and the Wounds obliterate all we once cherished—

as the Sparrow flies
it is not so very far away.
God cares about the sparrows and their flight,
and He sees when they fall.

I hope to have a faith like them
until the day when I at last journey
to the land from which no sparrow falls,
to the land where all the aches of love are softened
with the balm of gilead.

the fabric of love rustles, and wrinkles
bringing us closer than I ever thought possible—
and this ache?
perhaps it's just a folding, a bending and a breaking
to be brought near—to gather, and stitch together.

I hate the way this pain makes me understand
how I am loved.

yet, knowing this Divine Love
is all I ever wanted for my life
in the shadowlands.

acknowledgments

I want to say thank you to my 8ᵗʰ grade teacher, Miss Fawcett—for assigning me that poetry project and for believing in me even when all I wrote about was the joy of hot chocolate.

To my high school English teacher, Mrs. Ferrill—you taught me to love Shakespeare for the very fact that he gives us words for feelings we might not be able to name, or fully experience, otherwise. Your words gave me a goal to pursue in my own writing.

To my first creative writing teacher, Miss Griffin—you read some of my early work about my experience as a survivor of childhood sexual abuse and did not balk. Thank you for your early encouragement in my first serious attempts at poetry and for standing next to me as I stared into the black.

To my college professor and advisor, Sasha Steensen—you saw the Holy Spirit voice at work in my poetry, and you didn't call it the false cheerfulness of Hallmark. For that, I am forever grateful.

To Professor John Calderazzo—who told me, "Keep going on your writing, whatever it is." Thank you for always asking me what I was working on when you bumped into me while we were both getting coffee and pie.

To Eryn Lynum—who gave me the permission slip I needed to call myself a writer, as well as a mom, at the exact moment that I needed it. I thank God for your timely friendship.

To Anna—my mystical, magical, unicorn/babysitter/therapist/friend— I couldn't have survived the pandemic without you. You were a Godsend in every way possible, and you are, and will always be, part of our family.

To my most vocal cheerleader, Laura Albritton—your exuberance has driven this project from its inception. Thank you for being my Queen Anne. And to Andrew Albritton, a friend like a brother who tolerates my obscenely long hugs—thank you for holding us up during our dark days and for listening as I processed some of the loss I explore here in this book. With you, I know I'm still fun.

To my Instagram writer friends Sarah Southern, Sarah Westfall, Annelise Roberts, K.J. Ramsey, Liezel Graham, Careen Raynor, Steph Ebert, and so many others (you know who you are!)— your online friendship and words of encouragement over the years have lead to real-life growth for this writer, and I could not be more grateful for each and every one of you.

To my wonderful poetry friend turned editor, Elizabeth Berget—your thoughtful feedback has helped this work become the very best that it could be. Thank you for your belief in this project and your incredibly kind words along the way.

To my Spicy Dragon Ladies—thank you for laughing with me, for cheering on this project, and for helping me remember not to take myself too seriously. Book club night is my favorite.

To my dear friend Felicia—your daily texts through the ups and downs of preparing this manuscript (and just generally dealing with life) this past year have kept me anchored amidst the tossing sea. I am so glad I plopped my mat down next to yours in Pilates class, and that 10 years later God brought you back into my life. You are my angel.

To my parents, Allan and Joy Morton—thank you for being the first "beta readers" of the early version of this collection over two years ago and for cheering me on as I pursued making it a real thing out there in the world.

To my brother Luke Morton-Yates—you gave me the courage to pursue indie publication, and the kick in the pants I needed when you told me I owed it to myself to finish what I started—and to my sister-in-law Julie Morton-Yates who read the early version of this book and helped me especially with the order of the poems; I could not have done this without you both, and I hope that's totally obvious.

To my incomparable co-laborer, Bethanie Pack—thank you for contributing your listening ear as I explained my vision for the art for the book, and for so perfectly capturing the journey of the Sparrow in canvas and paint. You gave your heart and soul to each and every one of the pieces, and it shows.

To my husband Willy—you freed me up consistently and continually so I could finish this work, and it would not exist without you. Your belief in this project, and in me, is what has kept me going through all the times when I wanted to just throw in the towel. Thank you for being my person, my partner, and for holding onto me in the eye of every tornado.

To my kids, Ellie, Boaz, Isaiah, Nathan, and Jordan—loving you is the soul of this work, and the closest I have come to understanding what the Divine Love is like. I'm so grateful God gave you to me.

To King Jesus—whose love is the only reason I can still live, and breathe, and get up each day despite the ache—Thank you for caring about the sparrows.

And to You, Dear Reader—when you tell me that the blood I scribble on the page dries into the shape of words that mirror your very own ache, I feel this sense of purpose and peace. We are not alone—and as the Sparrow flies, perhaps the distance between us and all that we have loved and lost, is not so far after all.

about the author

Grace E. Kelley is a follower of Jesus, a wife, and mother of five, including a set of boy/girl twins. She graduated from Colorado State University with a Bachelors in Creative Writing and a double emphasis in Poetry and Creative Non-Fiction. She writes poetry and stories—both fictional and non-fictional, and occasionally enjoys the opportunity to speak. She is also a farmer, a foodie, an unrepentant mug addict, and a deep believer that incredible beauty can come from the compost heap.

You can find her writing on her Substack (graceekelley.substack.com). You can also follow her on Instagram and IG threads @graceekelleywrites.

as the Sparrow flies, is her debut collection—a long awaited dream fulfilled.

about the artist

Bethanie Pack is a contemporary landscape painter located in Denver, Colorado. She began her art career as an abstract artist fascinated with the challenge of creating form from the formless—asking questions such as "what is the color of innocence?" or "how can line depict ache or desperation?" This fascination with abstraction and mark-making followed Bethanie into her current representational landscape work, begging her to consider the intangible feelings a person experiences in nature, such as awe and wonder, when making decisions on form and color.

You can check out more of Bethanie's work at her website bethaniepack.com.

The Pucusana Project is working to alleviate poverty in Pucusana Peru by providing quality educational opportunities, creating programs to improve social issues and family dynamics, enabling financial stability through business training and cultivating a thriving Christian community through discipleship, worship and church planting.

Go to https://www.pucusanaproject.org/ to learn more and to donate.

JOIN ALLI IN ALLEVIATING POVERTY IN PUCUSANA PERU TODAY!

LIFE for the INNOCENT

Life for the Innocent partners with communities to RESCUE, RESTORE AND RENEW children affected by human trafficking.

Their vision is to combat child trafficking in South Asia by bringing holistic opportunities for physical, emotional, and spiritual freedom to children rescued from sex, labor, or organ trafficking.

Go to https://lifefortheinnocent.org/to learn how you can make a difference in the life of a child today.

Join Laura in Rescuing Trafficked Children Today!

Printed in the USA
CPSIA information can be obtained
at www.ICGtesting.com
CBHW081722310124
3898CB00001B/1